The Outside Inn

by

George Ella Lyon

illustrated by

Vera Rosenberry

ORCHARD BOOKS   NEW YORK

Orchard Books, 95 Madison Avenue, New York, NY 10016

Manufactured in the United States of America. Printed by Barton
Press, Inc. Bound by Horowitz/Rae. Book design by Mina Greenstein.
The text of this book is set in 36 pt. ITC Modern No. 216 Medium.
The illustrations are watercolor and ink line, done by brush, and
reproduced in full color.

Hardcover   10   9   8   7   6   5   4   3   2
Paperback   10   9   8   7   6   5   4   3   2   1

Library of Congress Cataloging-in-Publication Data
Lyon, George Ella, date.
The Outside Inn / by George Ella Lyon ;
illustrations by Vera Rosenberry.   p.   cm.
Summary: The rhyming verse presents all sorts of "appetizing" meals to
be had outdoors, including "puddle ink to drink," "gravel crunch for
lunch," and "worms and dirt for dessert."
ISBN 0-531-05936-7 (tr.)   ISBN 0-531-08536-8 (lib.)
ISBN 0-531-07086-7 (pbk.)
[1. Stories in rhyme.   2. Humorous stories.]
I. Rosenberry, Vera, ill.   II. Title.
PZ8.3.L9893Ou   1991   [E]—dc20   90-14285

For Kathleen Sterling
poet, teacher, friend
—G.E.L.

For Raman —V.R.

Welcome to The Outside Inn
where good times and good food begin.
What'll you have? What'll it be?
I'm your waiter. Just ask me.

What's for breakfast?

Ants
with
ketchup.

What's to drink?

Puddle ink.

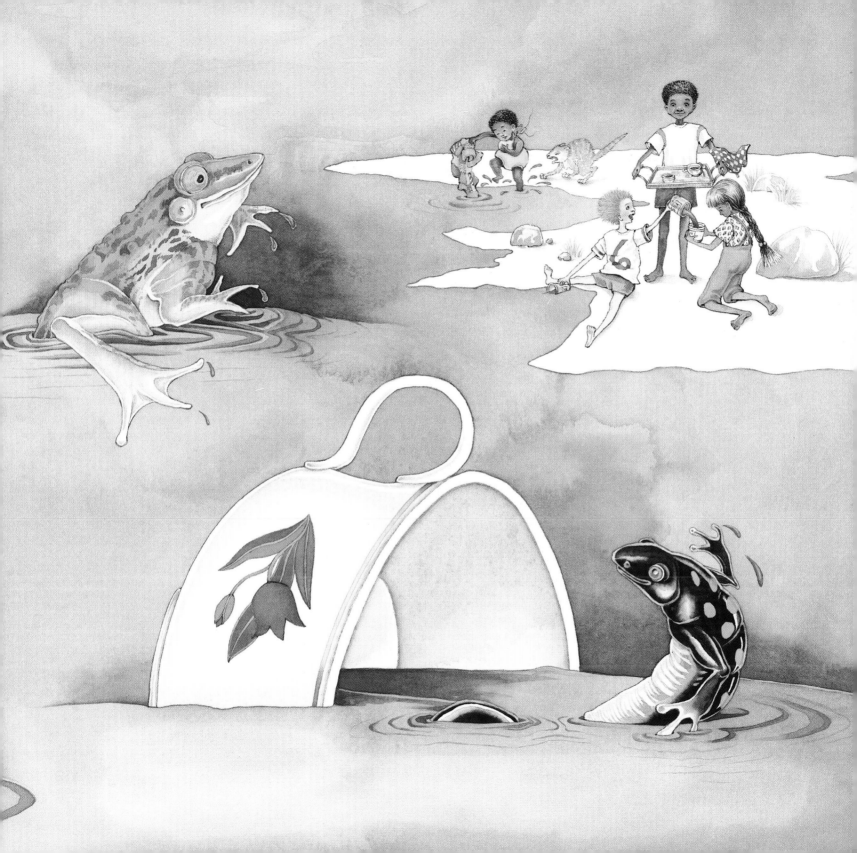

What's for snack?

Slugs in a sack.

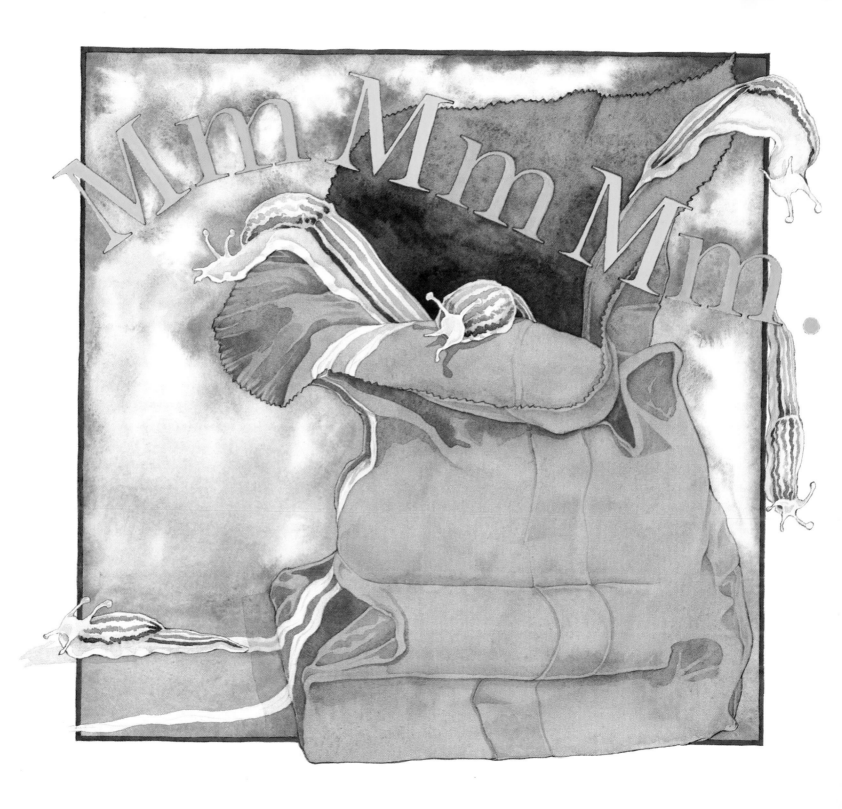

What's for lunch?

Gravel crunch.

What's for treat?

Caterpillar feet.

What's for tea?

A
sowbug
and
a flea.

Yum
Yum.
Yum
Yum.

What's for dinner?

Mud-pie thinner.

What's

for

dessert?

Worms

and

dirt.

WORMS

and

DIRT

???

Squirm in your spoon
and _**wriggle**_ at your chin.
Meals that crawl
from The Outside Inn!

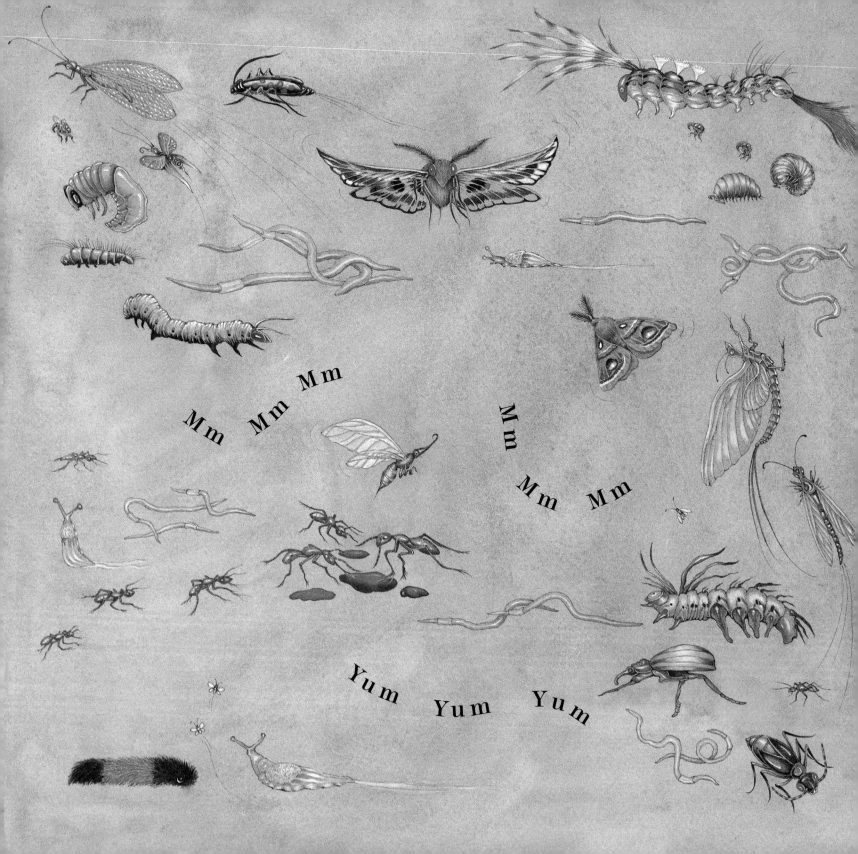

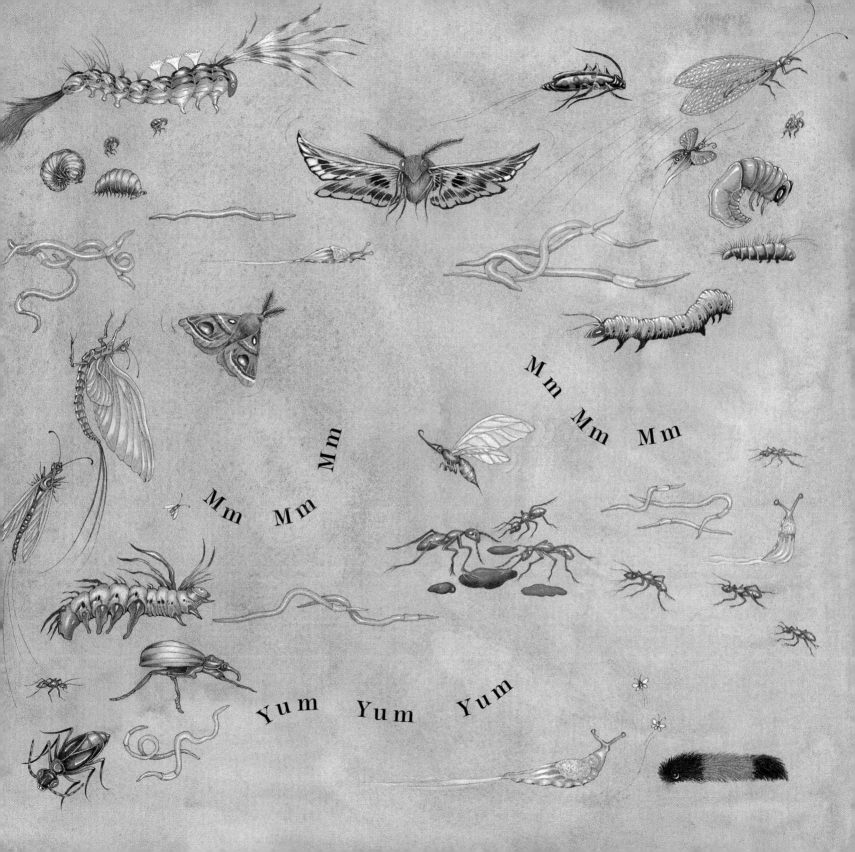